Whimsical Musings

& other spontaneous thoughts

Vanessa van der Baan

/ BookLeaf
Publishing

India | USA | UK

Made with ❤ on the BookLeaf Publishing Platform
www.bookleafpub.in
www.bookleafpub.com

Dedication

To all the people that made me, me. I love you all.

Preface

I thought I'd challenge myself to feel my world through words and to share them here.

Acknowledgements

I would like to sincerely thank everyone who inspires and supports me in all my creative endevours. Especially my family, Scott, Indigo and Clover, my mom, my brother and his wonderful family who I love, and all of my amazing friends who are all more special to me than you know!

1. A love letter to the last outdoor shower of summer....

Its weightless touch wraps its warm tendrils around me,
a dizzy, mushy, warm hug
Made evermore precious by its fleeting existence
Desperation, knowing too soon its over
Though pummeled, I feel buoyant
I dance to its primal song
My need to feel grows urgent,
like the last kiss of a fleeing lover
But this will end by my own hand
My need porous as a sponge
and wild as a summer storm,
basking in perfection
until I reach beyond all instinct
and twist the faucet off.

2. Decisions

Turnbuckle conundrum
about the size of time
How'd you negotiate
and walk the thin red line
Always answers,
always questions,
ricochet around
Your conscience feels,
inertia reels,
your feet can't leave the ground
Who's to say you've done it right,
the 'what ifs' shout so loud
Who's to say you'd recognize
yourself amongst a crowd
Things that used to mean a lot
shelved safely in your mind
To contemplate the path you took
on this ride steering blind

3. The temperate descent of the zinnia

Like brilliant fireworks on a summer day
Caught in an overstretched moment....
sustaining but fading ever so slowly,
as the long warm days slip past their season
and welcome falls cool handshake.
Tipped with drained color,
but still sustenance,
the bumblebees seem insatiable at their fall feast.
The stems, silent and loyal soldiers of the earth,
still standing tall without recoil.
Even as they die,
their legs, stiff in the browning tide,
hold strong, unwavering,
the unfurled prize held high as a last beacon of pride.
A jewel in the monotony of dying pigments
A crisping flicker bobbing on a cooling breeze,
that once baked juicily in the suns hot glory.
A speck of brilliant perfection,

If only for a breath in the sprawling melody of natures ensemble.

4. Little dream

Little dream,
always there by my side,
little dream
Always felt but not seen
In a way,
things distort through your screen,
little dream
Always pushing me towards what you see
On the way I get caught up in me
Holding on to you more than you know
How I reach towards you needing to grow
Little dream,
by your clues sometimes I feel close
But you blur as I near,
still I try to see clear
taunting with visions verbose
Little dream,
someday I will stand at your side
You'll surrender your title with pride
For the path will have been steep,

a promise that you keep,
to follow my own little dream

5. Unconscious

Warm enough to be a cool breeze the air blows,
tiny waves lapping steadily by its side.
Boats bobble carelessly as the water, which has already
reached its summer peak, cools lazily.
Grasses bend gently as if dancing their farewell to
summer.
There is an invisible anticipation building.
There is change tickling the surfaces, from air to sea to
skin.
There is a vastness to this, a direct order.
The things that we do not control are changing, and in
turn, so will we.
We think,
but the expanse that cradles us prevails without thought
or agenda.
Its meaning is meaningless.
Our importance just a figment of a delicate imagination.

6. Great Mysteries

Apple jack, roof rack,
where do seas collide?
Beyond the bridge of pleasantries,
surrounded by a pride.
Hay bale, banana cage,
making crazy cool.
Swap your neighbor for a flag,
forget the golden rule.
Hogs boot, hoof light,
why the sour smell?
The pageantry has take reign,
canaries aren't well.
Rummy bog, icy paper,
find your feisty pen.
Bellyaching won't undo,
Sweet fractures meant to mend.

7. Acoustic hysteria

Noise,
polluting the pleasure of sound.
Aggressive, loud, uncaring,
made from the same fabric,
but with a less refined nap.
Like sandpaper grating on the soul
A million spinning hooks,
pulling you every which way,
but nowhere you wanted to be.
Bombardment,
not asking for permission, nor caring.
Enveloping in dissonance.
A thousand false starts.
An outburst lacking manners.
Pad the walls,
I need to think,
in silence.

8. October lullaby

Angry gray clouds grab down to the dark sea with
hungry fingers from the sky above
They seem to stir a frantic tide below,
percolating a seasonal angst with haunting intention,
emboldening and inviting the dormant autumnal
crescendo to awake
Tree bows nod in consent, laying a bejeweled carpet at
the feet of Mother Nature
Darkening days descend,
stealing last light with greedy anticipation
Echos of wayward geese resound,
conducting the cacophony of dusks concerto
The requiem transcends, punctuated by rustling leaves,
lending their crisp timbre to the longing autumn night
Darkness in its totality envelopes what's left of the days
reluctance in its velvet grip,
swallowed whole
Nights foreboding lullabies
Enchant the restless void

9. Mirages of you

In the mirrors of my mind,
I see the silhouette of time,
shaped, as only you could be
effervescent youth to tease
We thought forever shone past stars
Past milestones, past lives and wars
But turns out to include us too,
as time slipped by and so did you
I think of you with wistful ease
A moment traveled on a breeze
When endless futures held our hands
And time surrendered to our whims
Sweet memories I'll hold for now
Of times that don't exist somehow
How silently we drift away
While banking on another day
That sometimes comes
And sometimes not
And somehow that moment
Was all that we got

A piece of me
You'll always fill
As we skip past forever
With stories to tell

10. Written in the stars

What if the stars, are held up by strings,
and wishes are tossed from the bottom of springs?
What if I wished,
on one just to see you?
And all the impossible,
turned out to be true
What if we found all desires abundant?
Would we grow tired,
And fickle,
despondent?
What if we landed right back in our past?
Would we know better?
Moments don't last
What if we didn't drift far from our start?
We wouldn't be missing
A piece of our heart

11. In the Depths

Sunken
Like a pile of rocks sitting in stillness at the bottom of a
dark lake
We're all hurting
Glimpses revealed between half smiles and sarcasm
An ever searing burn
Sometimes igniting you to strive,
sometimes leaving you smoldering in the ashes
Balanced delicately between extremes
It's nothing and everything and it feels so heavy
We bear this alone through the crowds
We bear this because we feel deeply
We bear the burden,
a gift of humility

12. Saturated

The rain falls down,
with the gravity of gravity,
a melancholy melody,
a softly spreading fallacy,
to lose me in myself

It pulls me in
a void I had avoided,
over thoughts
I knew collided
It's uncomfortable
to lose me in myself

But I'm still slipping
as I'm gripping,
to the dry room
where I'm sitting,
trying desperately
to grasp what's really real

I hold my breath,
I try to feel,
I try to breathe,
the air I steal
It makes more sense,
my anchor thrown,
past dampness soaked,
I'm in my home

The day is long,
the rain makes sound,
I close my eyes,
it's pouring down

13. Two peas

Each tiny little part of you
invades me like you're super glue
With glitter sparkles all around
A dazzling, daring, deafening sound
With an unrelenting magnetic cling
We're bound by space and moons that sing
Days craze by with senseless fun
We tiptoe together and bury the sun

14. Just a Little Longer

I wake from a world of crisscrossed carnivals
entwined in forgotten tapestries
A notion blowing by on the breeze
A night spent with strangers
only strange from times long embrace
It waves, daring me to remember
Familiar faces sharpen
from the hazy blur of a dizzying kaleidoscope
Fantastical theatrics lure me onward through richly
imagined realities
I feel, I smell, I see, in a nocturnal parade of spectacular
impossibilities
Their improbability sneaks undetected
beneath my incapacitated consciousness
A world alive inside me and yet somewhere way beyond
me
Always cut too short
I drag my eyelids open

15. Sandcastles

I spotted the sandcastle,
abandoned, alone,
a bit of a challenge,
enticing, it shone
On the shoreline
surrounded by stones,
in need of repair,
the needy sea moaned
It seemed so beautiful,
seaside in the sun
I got to work patching
and building, so fun
The tide stepped up to lend a hand
So I worked twice as hard,
piling sand
The give and take,
a jeering game,
was only fun for the waves that came.
For I piled and piled to no avail
Anyone could see I was setup to fail.

The fight I fought was once just play,
It had turned at some point,
I cannot say.
I knew I couldn't possibly win,
but I'd play until my needs wore thin.
I needed a break,
the situation was dire,
and I left defeated,
past time to retire.
So why did I think I could wrangle the tide,
Born wild, its nature to never subside.

16. Only Sounds

A blade so sharp,
in a word spoken
With the carelessness of a child
and the intention of a marksman.
The shields surround me.
They rarely come down,
and for a while they will hold.
I know
It is the same battle
Words slammed and speared
An invisible attack,
perhaps an imaginary one I tell myself.
But beneath the armor my soul stings.
My body quickens
My stomach turns
I shake
If I attach no meaning,
these sounds should do no harm.
They shouldn't hurt
I shouldn't writhe

But somehow with complete fortification they have hit
their mark
again

17. enough

To cross every t
and dot every i
is already too much
so why did I try?

18. No. 2 pencil

Sliding like the slick back of a shiny porpoise,
It squirms in squiggly loops,
laughing in lolling echos,
as it glazes the page with its grey veneer
To tell a tale with texture and tooth
To feel the words pressed singularly, selectively,
into the soft belly
of a blank page
A transfer
Energy igniting and immortalizing
legends upon a ledger

19. Unconditional Love

Deep low vibrations
Breaths of raw desire,
with a pleasure so complete
Mysteriously knowing eyes, rolling in unquenchable
ecstasy
Fur as black as a velvet eclipse
Rubbing needy whiskers,
impatiently, forcefully,
thirsty for touch
A small soft body with its downy warmth
nestled fluidly into an unimagined crook
Completing me,
fitting flawlessly
The puzzle piece
I never knew I was without

20. A house once a home

It is empty now,
not of treasure and accumulation,
of that it is full,
but of spirit, unique and forceful,
essential,
a placeholder of existence.
Possessions remain,
illusions of needs that once mattered,
now forgotten without notice.
Life is the collector of time.
Mementos, the footnote of indelible memories,
touchstones,
but little more.
It is the moments though that are treasures within me,
they create me,
they become me
Flavors that make life worth living
Saturating your tongue,
electrifying your mind,
they tickle your skin like a silky breeze.

Irreplicable aromas wistfully transporting you,
one last time.
Invisible,
these are the things that shine brightest.
Stars of the soul that keep sparkling beyond their
numbered days.
A thousand collected snapshots parade through my
mind, but I can feel the void,
it is empty now

21. Steal this poem

Isn't everything we say, cliché
Painted already on a previous day
To a previous crowd
With previous thoughts
With passion and patience,
and stories we're taught?
How are we to be different this time?
When ages have happened
And thoughts aren't mine
They are a mix of days that passed
Of countless encounters
And hearts of glass
What are the chances of a novel idea?
Probably zero
at least that what I hear

www.ingramcontent.com/pod-product-compliance
Lightning Source LLC
Chambersburg PA
CBHW051000030426
42339CB00007B/417